Little Miss Tr

M

Inspired by life with the Mr. Men
Illustrated by Adam Hargreaves

Men can never own too
many cordless drills.
No one knows why.

Mr. Busy

Men don't get colds . . . they get flu.

Mr. Sneeze

Never try to part a man from his sofa.

Mr. Grumpy

To him exotic food is keeping the gherkin.

Mr. Greedy

All men think they are Mr. Funny.

Few women admit their age.
Fewer men act it.

Mr. Silly

Men get enough exercise just
pushing their luck.

**Little Miss
Lucky**

Mr. Mischief

Men seem to have missed some of the steps on the evolutionary ladder.

Mr. Tickle

Women would love to take
men seriously . . . but then
there are comedy ties.

Mr. Dizzy

Men are like high heels – easy to walk on once you get the hang of it.

Mr. Small

It's not that women can't read maps, it's that men take wrong turnings.

Mr. Muddle   **Little Miss Wise**

Never let a man's mind wander . . . it's too little to be let out on its own.

Mr. Silly

Men are all the same, they just have different faces so you can tell them apart.

Women don't make fools of men – most of them are the do-it-yourself types.

Mr. Funny

**The best way to get a man
to do something is to
suggest he is too old for it.**

Mr. Strong

So many men, so few
who can afford me.

Mr. Mean

Little Miss Splendid

What do you do if
your man walks out?
Shut the door.

Little Miss Lucky

Men are like computers –
hard to figure out and never
have enough memory.

Mr. Forgetful

Don't imagine you can change a male of the species, unless he's in nappies.

Mr. Lazy   **Little Miss Magic**

Men's idea of fun isn't necessarily the same as women's.

Mr. Noisy   **Little Miss Splendid**

So many men . . . so many
reasons not to date them.

greedy…grumpy…noisy…lazy…mean.

If they can put a man on the moon, they should be able to put them all there.

**Little Miss
Curious**

**Men are very clear on
what is the human race's
greatest achievement.**

Mr. Lazy

Men wear their hair 3 ways:
parted, unparted & departed.

Mr. Fussy   **Mr. Clumsy**   **Mr. Worry**

For men, the concept of commitment does not extend further than the football field.

Mr. Lazy

TOP 10 THINGS MEN KNOW ABOUT WOMEN:

1.
2.
3.
4.
5.

6.
7.
8.
9
10.

Mr. Wrong

When a man says 'It would take too long to explain,' he really means, 'I have no idea how it works.'

Mr. Clever

When it comes to multi-tasking,
men tend to stick to the basic three:
chewing, looking, sitting.

Mr. Greedy   Mr. Slow   Mr. Lazy

**Contrary to popular belief,
Mr. Perfect DOES NOT EXIST.**

Little Miss Brainy

Boys will be boys . . .

Mr. Nosey

. . . unfortunately.